Mel Bay Presents

Easy Celtic Harp Solos

Irish   Manx   Bretton   Hebridean
Scottish   Cornish   Welsh

by Star Edwards

1 2 3 4 5 6 7 8 9 0

Visit us on the Web at www.melbay.com — E-mail us at email@melbay.com

TABLE OF CONTENTS

Berrey Dhone .... Manx 3
The Blackbird .... Welsh 4
Bonnie Laddie, Highland Laddie .... Scottish 6
Carolan's Fancy (Planxty Safaigh) .... Irish 8
The Castle of Neath .... Welsh 9
Cumberland Reel .... Scottish 10
Gentle Maiden .... Irish 11
The Harp of Dunvegan .... Hebridean 12
I Love My Love .... Cornish 13
Lullaby (Suo-Gan) .... Welsh 14
The Maid of Llanwellyn .... Welsh 15
The Marigold .... Cornish 16
Minstrel Boy .... Irish 17
Mylecharaine .... Manx 18
My Love She's But a Lassie Yet .... Scottish 20
Pardon Spezed .... Bretton 21
Pet of the Pipers .... Irish 22
Planxty Charles Coote .... Irish 23
Quinze Marins .... Bretton 24
Scottish Reform .... Scottish 26
The Sea Invocation .... Manx 27
Tam Glen .... Scottish 28
Tri Martolod .... Bretton 30
Weavers March .... Scottish 32
Welsh Carol .... Welsh 34
Song Notes 36

Berrey Dhone

Manx

The Blackbird

Welsh

Bonnie Laddie, Highland Laddie

Scottish

CAROLAN'S FANCY

Irish

The Castle of Neath

Flip up C lever in the 10th measure

Welsh

CUMBERLAND REEL

Moderate

GENTLE MAIDEN

Irish

The Harp of Dunvegan

Hebridean

I Love My Love

Cornish

LULLABY (SUO-GAN)

Welsh

The Maid of Llanwellyn

Welsh

The Marigold

Flip B lever up in measure 12

Cornish

Minstrel Boy

Irish

MYLECHARAINE

Slow
Flip up levers on A

Manx

My Love She's But a Lassie Yet

Scottish

Pardon Spezed

Bretton

PET OF THE PIPERS

Irish

PLANXTY CHARLES COOTE

Irish

QUINZE MARINS

Slow

Bretton

SCOTTISH REFORM

Scottish

The Sea Invocation

Manx

Tam Glen

Scottish

This page has been
left blank to avoid
awkward page turns

Tri Martolod

Bretton

WEAVERS MARCH

Scottish

*This page has been
left blank to avoid
awkward page turns*

Welsh Carol

Welsh

Song Notes

Berrey Dhone (Brown Betty the Witch) - Traditional Manx
This song is about a woman who follows Berrey Dhone down to the Clieau Rea bay where she sees her turn into a seal woman

> Tir'ed out, Berrey Dhone? O, you look'd cool,
> In the dark grassy glades down by Barrule
> Forth you went leading us, lifting the hill
> All the night far from home, fooling us still...

The Blackbird (Y Fwyalchen) - In the words of this song, a lover tells the bird to take his message of love to his sweetheart. This image introduced into this song is known as *Llateiaeth*.

Bonnie Laddie - Highland Laddie -- Scottish song about going off to war, promising his loved one he would honor the "tartan plaid and Highland trew"

Carolan's Fancy/Planxty Safaigh - Irish song by O'Carolan, written to his patron. "A planxty is a tune (an English name, 'pleraca,' as the Irish name) composed in honor of one's patron or hospitable entertainers." It is also a harp-tune of a sportive and animated character..." (Carolan - The Life, Times and Music of an Irish Harper)

The Castle of Neath (Castle Nedd) This air comes from the vale of Neath in southern Wales. This castle, built in the 12th century was one of the minor Norman castles in the lordship of Glamorgan. It was destroyed by Llywelyn ap Iorwerth in 1231 and then rebuilt in the 14th century. The Normans chose this strategic spot guarding the river crossing for a stronghold.

Cumberland Reel - Traditional Scottish. From the Carlton Collection of Easy Scottish Dance Music.

Gentle Maiden - Traditional Irish, ancient air from the Bunting collection. Bunting obtained this air in Dublin in 1839. He gave it the name *As fada annso me*, (or *Long Am I Here* or *The Gentle Maiden*.) Although there is much dispute whether Bunting considered this tune English or Irish.

The Harp of Dunvegan - Traditional Hebridean. Much like the song *The Minstrel Boy*, this song recollects the glory of the harps "luring sung story by the graves of Shil Leoid"...(the clan Macleods). Dunvegan is a castle on the Isle of Skye, that has managed to be occupied by the same family, the Macleods, over the centuries. Dunvegan was also easily defended and it was probably a strongpoint for the Vikings from whom the Macleod's claim descent. The Clans gather here from all over the world and admire the fabled Fairy Flag that protects them and the Chief from danger. Chief Dame Flora who passed away in 1976 encouraged all Macleods to visit Dunvegan.

I Love My Love - Traditional Cornish melody (also known as *The Maid in Bedlam*). The story of a woman whose lover is sent out to sea. She is put in a place for the sick called Bedlam, where she is bound in chains, but continues to sing "I love my love because I know, my love loves me..." When he returns from sea, and finds out she went to Bedlam, he comes to rescue her. He sings to her, "I love my love because I know, my love loves me."

Lullaby (Suo-gan) - Traditional Welsh Lullaby
> "...Through your dreaming you are beaming, oh so purely now my store,
> You must see your angel surely, smiling through heavens open door..."

Maid of Llanwellyn - Welsh song about a poor country man whose life is made proud, when the maid of Llanwellyn smiles sweetly on him.

The Marigold - Traditional Cornish. This song is about a sea fight of a ship called the Marigold with Captain Sir

Thomas Merrifield of Bristol, against Turkish rovers. This story was written down by Davies Gilbert, the Cornish historian in 1830.

Minstrel Boy - Irish song from the traditional arrangement *The Moreen*. About the glory of long ago.
"'Land of song!' said the warrior-bard,
Though all the world betrays thee,
One sword, at least, thy rights shall guard,
One faithful harp shall praise thee."

Mylecharaine - Traditional Manx song. This song tells the story of how the dowry was started for the first time on the Isle of Mann. Mylecharaine is a conversation between a daughter and her father. She criticizes him for the questionable means to provide a dowry, namely murdering a rich man.

My Love She's But a Lassie Yet - Traditional Scottish, Robert Burns song. This air is known as *Lady Badinscoth's Reel* and *Miss Farquharson's Reel*. Many other versions of the same song exist. An altered version of Wordsworth's *A Famous Man was Robin Hood* was also sung to the same air.

Pardon Spezed - Traditional Bretton song

Pet of the Pipers - Traditional Irish jig

Planxty Charles Coote - Irish song about one of O'Carolan's patrons.

Quinze Marins - Traditional Bretton

Scottish Reform - From the Carlton Collection of Easy Scottish Dance Music.

The Sea Invocation - Traditional Manx
Heavenly wind my loves on the brine, Ho ro y ree y ro, Ho ro y ree y ro
Make the weather calm and fine, Ho ro y ree y ro, Ho ro y ree y ro
Give him luck and joy always, Health and peace and length of days
Ho ro y ree y ro, Ho ro y ree y ro

Tam Glen - Traditional Scottish, Robert Burns tune. Written by Burns in 1788, it tells the tale of a woman in love with Tam Glen. Verses in this song refer to old Scottish folklore and superstitions, such as St. Valentines Dealing and Halloween. St. Valentine Dealing was an old custom where the lads and lassies would draw lots with names of their sweethearts for the following year. On Halloween the superstition is explained in the song that one would go to a running spring where "3 lairds" lands meet and dip your left shirt sleeve in. Go to bed in sight of a fire and hang your wet sleeve near the fire to dry. Lie awake, and close to midnight, an apparition will come and turn the sleeve to dry the other side. The apparition would give counsel to the maid in love to marry her Tam Glen.

Tri Martolod - Traditional Bretton. The title means 3 sailors.

The Weaver's March - Scottish tune, same as the *Gallant Weaver*. From Aird's Selection of Scots Airs of 1784. In 1786 Robert Burns' sweetheart, "Bonnie Jean," went to live with her parents in the town of Parsley. Two months later, he learned she danced with a weaver (Robie Wilson) to whom she was to marry. Burns wrote this poetic revenge for Jean.

Welsh Carol - (Mae'r Flwyddyn yn Marw T on Garol) Welsh traditional with English words by Walter Maynard.
"The old year is dying fast, dying away,
a full cloudy sunset has clos'd its last day,
The night winds are sighing, its last hour is fled,
The bells have ceas'd ringing. The old year is dead."

Star Edwards

Star Edwards' musical influences range from church music, Beatles, Dylan, Baez to international folk dance music. Guitar, psaltery, recorder and dulcimer were a precursor to discovering her Irish background which fueled her passionate journey with the Celtic harp. Star studied under Therese Schroeder-Sheker and Laurie Riley in the early '80s. Her professional career includes a performance on the Perry Mason episode, The Case of the Skin Deep Scandal, and The Princess and the Dwarf movie starring Warwick Davis and John Rhyes-Davies. In 1983, Star established and directed the Colorado Folk Harp Society to promote an awareness of the harp to the community, which led to the annual presence of the Celtic harp at the Scottish Highland Games in Highlands Ranch, and an alluring appeal to the local Irish festivals. She resides in Denver, Colorado, teaching, recording and performing harp.

EXCELLENCE IN MUSIC